Let's Count the Elephants

To Parents: Ask your child, "How many elephants are on this page?"
You can extend the activity by asking your child to describe the elephant.
The stickers for this activity can be found at the front of the book.

Count the elephants. Place the same number of stickers on the plate.

2

Let's Count the Monkeys

Count the monkeys. Place the same number of stickers on the plates.

Let's Count the Rabbits

To Parents: If your child is confused about where to put the carrot stickers, explain that each rabbit should get one carrot sticker.

Sticker

Count the rabbits. Place the same number of stickers on the plates.

Let's Finish the Dog Picture

To Parents: With this activity, your child will practice matching a part of a picture with the whole picture. Call attention to the shapes of the stickers if your child is unsure about where to place them.

Place the tail and ear stickers on the dog. What sound does a dog make?

dog

Let's Find the Dogs

To Parents: First, ask your child to point to the dogs on the page. To extend the activity, point to another animal and ask, "What animal is this?" or ask other questions, such as, "Which animal has the shortest tail?"

Draw a circle around each dog.

dog

Let's Draw Stripes

To Parents: In this activity, your child will practice drawing short, straight lines, which is an important part of writing numbers and letters.

Draw stripes on the tiger.

• Example •

Let's Color the Cow

To Parents: Make sure your child chooses the same color as the rest of the cow's spots. This activity fosters your child's ability to pick matching colors.

Finish coloring the cow's spots. What sound does a cow make?

COW

Let's Help the Mouse

To Parents: In this activity, your child will practice using reasoning and problem-solving skills. Encourage your child to come to a complete stop at each split in the path and think about which direction to go.

Draw a path from ➡ to ➡ to get the mouse safely past the cat.

mouse

cat

Let's Draw Whiskers

To Parents: When your child sees a cat in real life, point and say, "That is a cat." Connecting the word with the real animal will help your child remember it.

Trace the lines to give the cat whiskers. Can you meow like a cat?

cat

Let's Help the Cat Find Its Food

To Parents: The maze is simple, but it is still important to praise your child when he or she reaches the end.

The cat is hungry. Trace a path along the footprints from ➡ to ➡ to help the cat reach its food.

cat

Let's Connect the Dots

To Parents: Encourage your child to count out loud while connecting the dots.

Connect the ● from ONE **1** ➡ TWO **2** ➡ THREE **3** . What is Elephant holding?

Let's Draw Zigzags

To Parents: Drawing short lines like the ones below is an important step toward writing numbers and letters correctly.

Trace the - - - - from ● to ● to give the dinosaurs spiky backs.

Let's Trace the Teeth

To Parents: These short zigzag lines may be difficult for your child to draw. On the top crocodile, encourage your child to pause at each point before changing direction. On the bottom crocodile, encourage your child to trace each set of teeth without stopping. It is okay if the lines are messy.

GOOD JOB!

Sticker

Trace the crocodile's teeth. They are sharp!

• Example •

Let's Draw Spirals

To Parents: In this activity, your child will trace spiral lines. It does not matter if he or she starts from the inside or the outside of the spiral. Let your child pick the color of the crayon or marker.

Trace the spiral shapes using any color you like.

Example

Let's Help the Bees

To Parents: This activity builds problem-solving skills.

Trace the dotted lines to help the bees get to the flowers.

Let's Help the Ants

To Parents: Remind your child to follow the dots of the same color from beginning to end. If your child is confused that two ants go into the same home, let him or her know that it is okay. Ants live together in large groups.

GOOD JOB!
Sticker

Trace the dotted lines to help the ants bring their food home.

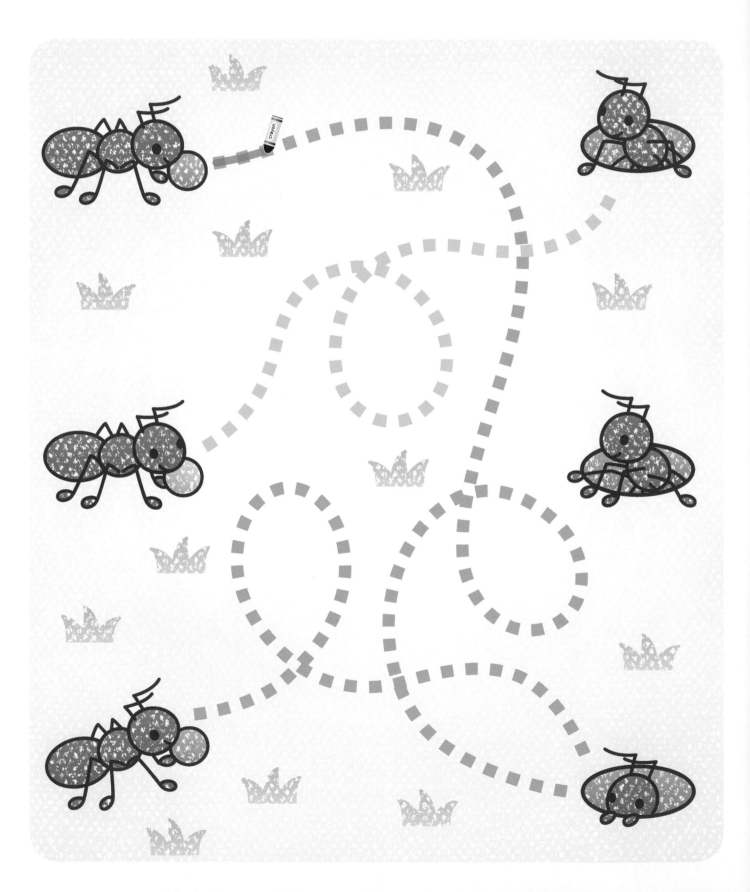

Let's Connect the Dots

To Parents: In this activity, your child will finish the picture by connecting the dots. Let your child know it is okay to draw as quickly or slowly as she or he is comfortable with.

Connect the dots from ● and ● to draw the rabbit's ears. Can you hop like a rabbit?

rabbit

Let's Color the Pigs

To Parents: Encourage your child to pick a color that matches the rest of the pig picture. To extend the learning, ask your child to describe the pig to you.

Finish coloring the pigs. Can you oink like a pig?

pig

Let's Find the Blue Fish

To Parents: To extend the activity, have your child count the blue, yellow, and pink fish.

GOOD JOB!

Sticker

Draw a circle around each blue fish.

Let's Find the Picture With More Rabbits

To Parents: In this activity, your child will compare quantities. It may be obvious without counting, but encourage your child to count each group of rabbits out loud before coloring the circle.

Count the rabbits in each picture. Using any color you like, color the ◯ next to the picture that has more rabbits.

Let's Find the Picture With More Cats

To Parents: This activity is designed to help children learn how to compare different quantities. Have your child point to and count each cat individually before comparing.

Count the cats in each picture. Using any color you like, color the ◯ next to the picture that has more cats.

Let's Find the Picture With More Mice

To Parents: When there are more items in a picture, it is even more important for your child to count each animal individually rather than rely on intuition.

Count the mice in each picture. Using any color you like, color the ◯ next to the picture that has more mice.

Let's Find the Picture With More Birds

To Parents: If your child has difficulty with this activity, encourage him or her to draw a line from each bird in the top picture to a bird in the bottom picture.

Count the birds in each picture. Using any color you like, color the ◯ next to the picture that has more birds.

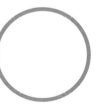

Let's Go Through the Maze

To Parents: This activity teaches problem solving and develops the skills needed for good writing. Remind your child to draw in the yellow pathways and not to go over the orange lines.

Draw a path through the banana from  to  .

Let's Find the Match

Which animal does this shadow belong to? Draw a line to the matching animal below.

cat　　　mouse　　　dog

Let's Draw Stripes

To Parents: Drawing lines like these develops the skills needed for good handwriting. It is okay if your child's stripes go a little bit outside the lines.

GOOD JOB!

Sticker

Draw stripes on the zebras.

• Example •

Let's Make Animals

To Parents: Once your child has completed this activity, show him or her how to disconnect the paper strips and fold them the other way to reveal other animals. Encourage your child to tell a story using these animals as characters.

1 ✂ Cut along the thick gray lines.

2 ✂ Cut slits along the short orange lines.

Turn the page for more instructions.

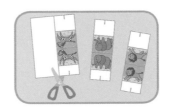
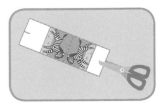

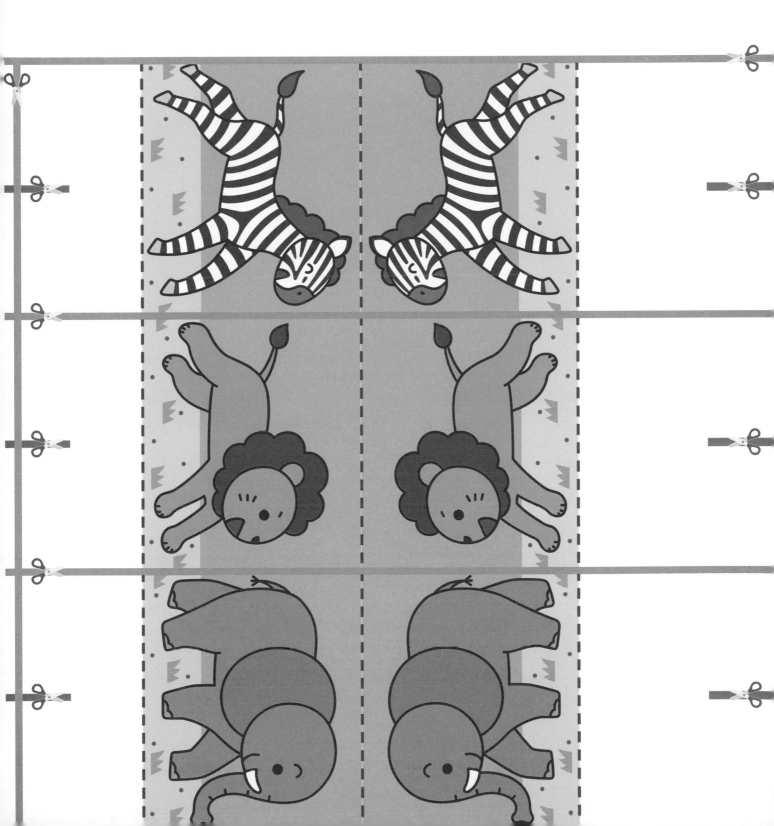

3 – – –Fold each paper strip along the dotted pink lines to make a triangle.

4 Connect the triangles using the slits you cut along the orange lines.

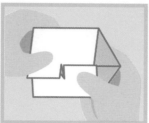
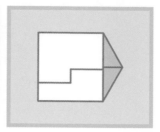

Let's Connect the Dots

To Parents: To spark your child's imagination before beginning this activity, ask, "What do you think you will see when you connect the dots?"

Connect the ● from ONE 1 → TWO 2 → THREE 3. What is on Monkey's head?

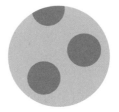

Let's Compare the Number of Bananas

To Parents: Make sure your child counts the bananas at the starting point before going through the maze.

GOOD JOB!
Sticker

Count the bananas at the start of the maze. Then, draw a path from ➡ to ➡ by going through groups of bananas that have the same number of bananas as the first group.

Let's Color the Bird and the Flowers

To Parents: Suggest that your child use the same color she or he sees in the example box below. The little bird has a simple shape, but coloring the dandelions may be more difficult. If your child is coloring outside of the lines, encourage her or him to slow down.

GOOD JOB!

Sticker

Color the bird and the dandelions.

• Example •

Let's Compare the Quantity

To Parents: Drawing lines between objects in two different groups makes it easier to see which quantity is greater.

 Sticker

Draw a line from each dog to one bowl of food. Then, count the dogs and the bowls of food. Compare the number of dogs to the number of bowls of dog food.

Are there more dogs or bowls of dog food? Place the sticker on the correct .

Let's Draw Lines

To Parents: This activity combines drawing straight and curved lines. It exercises fine motor skills and improves focus.

GOOD JOB!
Sticker

33

Trace the ----- from ● to ● to help the animals get their treats.

Let's Draw Loops

To Parents: In the first part of this activity, your child can follow the gray guidelines to trace the looping lines. But in the second part, your child will draw the looping lines freehand.

Using any color you like, trace the looping pattern on the top sheep. Then, draw it on the bottom sheep.

• Example •

Let's Complete the Maze

To Parents: Make sure your child understands that he or she should not draw over the dark purple lines. This activity builds problem-solving skills and helps to develop the ability to look ahead.

Draw a path through the grapes from  to ➡.

Let's Color by Number

To Parents: This activity aims to improve your child's number-recognition skills. When your child has finished coloring, say, "What animal do you see?"

Find all the shapes with a ^{FOUR} **4** . Color them using any color you like.

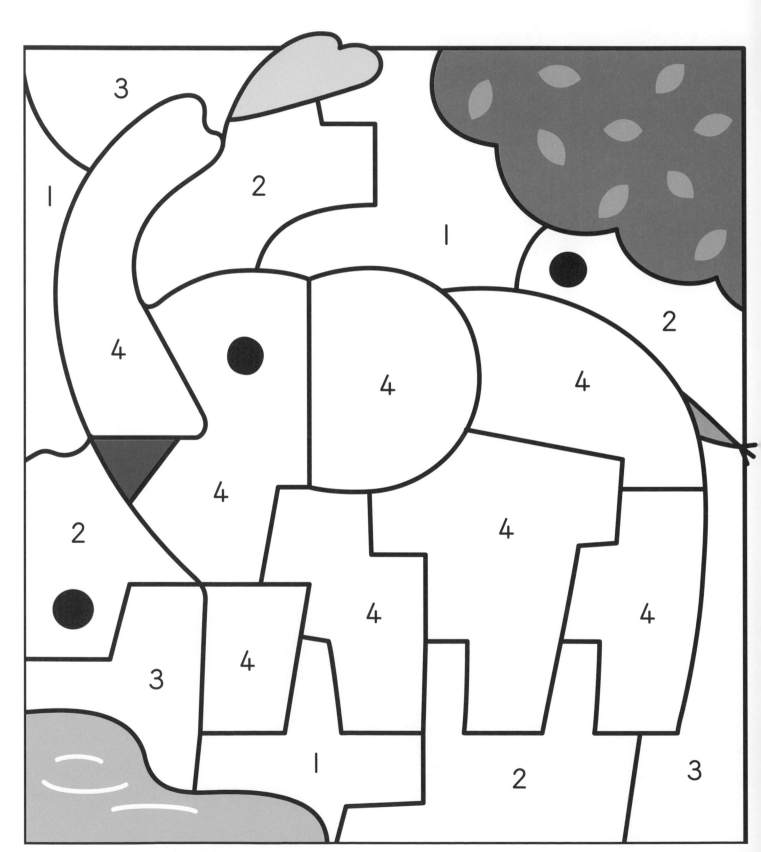

Let's Finish the Pig Picture

To Parents: The stickers for this activity are in the front of the book. Call attention to the shapes of the stickers if your child is unsure about where to place them.

Place the nose and tail stickers on the pig.

pig

Let's Follow the Rabbits

To Parents: Explain to your child that he or she can only move through the maze by passing through the openings in the blue lines. Extend the activity by asking your child to count the different animals.

GOOD JOB!

Sticker

Follow the rabbits to get from ➡ to ➡.

rabbit   cat   dog

Let's Connect the Dots

To Parents: Show your child the picture in the example box. Then ask your child to pay attention to the location, length, and direction of each line needed to re-create the picture. Your child can match the colors in the example box or pick others.

GOOD JOB!

Sticker

Draw lines from ● to ● to make pictures of birds that match the examples.

• Example •

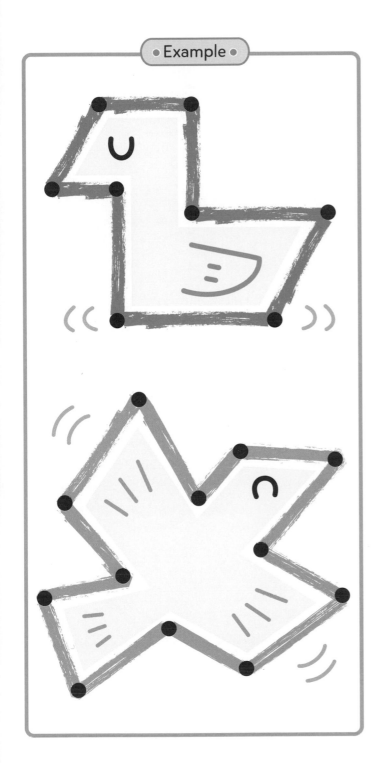

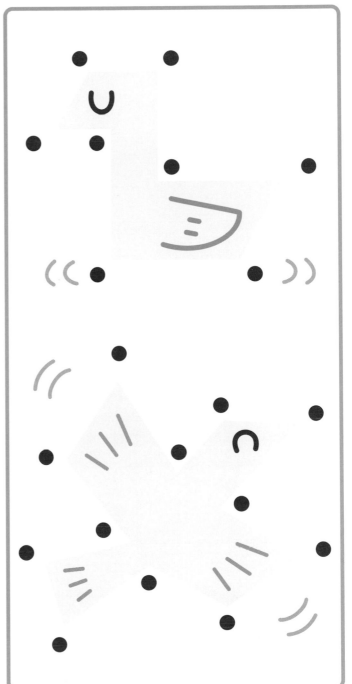

Let's Color the Fishbowl

To Parents: Encourage your child to place the fish stickers anywhere he or she would like, but suggest that they be in the fishbowl.

Finish coloring the fishbowl. Then, place the fish stickers wherever you want.

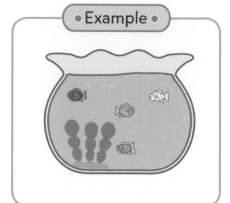
• Example •

Let's Trace the Fish

To Parents: Drawing boosts concentration skills, creativity, and fine motor control. To extend the activity, ask your child if she or he would like to draw more fish or add more bubbles.

Trace the outlines of the fish using any color you like.

Let's Count the Cats

To Parents: You may want to advise your child to mark each cat as it is counted. That way, he or she will avoid miscounting.

Count the cats. Then, color the same number of ◯ at the bottom of the page. Use any color you like.

Let's Count the Rabbits

To Parents: Here, your child will identify specific objects within a group of similar objects. This activity focuses on your child's observational skills.

GOOD JOB!

Sticker

Rabbits love carrots. Do you? Draw a circle around each rabbit that is eating a carrot.

carrot

Let's Draw the Horse's Mane

To Parents: Let your child decide how to draw the horse's mane. It does not have to match the example. If your child is unfamiliar with how a horse sounds and acts, watch a video online together.

GOOD JOB!

Sticker

Draw the horse's mane. Can you pretend to be a horse?

horse

• Example •

Let's Follow the Horse

To Parents: This activity teaches problem solving and develops the skills needed for good writing.

Draw a path through the maze from ➡ to ➡. Make the noises of the animals you pass along the way.

Let's Trace the Chick and the Egg

To Parents: Drawing circles, ovals, and curved lines will help boost your child's fine motor coordination and handwriting skills.

Trace the outline of the chick and the egg. Use any color you like.

• Example •

Let's Match the Tail

GOOD JOB!

Sticker

Which animal does this tail belong to? Draw a line to connect the tail to its match.

pig

cow

horse

Let's Connect the Dots

To Parents: In this activity, your child will practice drawing diagonal lines and straight lines. Activities like this increase your child's ability to focus.

Connect the ● from **ONE** 1 ➡ **TWO** 2 ➡ **THREE** 3 ➡ **FOUR** 4 ➡ **FIVE** 5 by drawing lines.

Let's Count the Squirrels

To Parents: To extend the activity, ask your child to count the acorns.

Count the squirrels. Then, color the same number of ◯ at the bottom of the page.
Use any color you like.

Let's Trace the Camel's Humps

To Parents: Guide your child to follow the curved gray lines over the animals' humps. Line-drawing skills like these are needed for proper handwriting.

Trace the camels' humps using any color you like.

Let's Help Rabbit

To Parents: Make sure your child counts the number of flowers at each split in the path before choosing which way to go.

GOOD JOB!

Sticker

Draw a path from ➡ to ➡ to help Rabbit collect flowers for her mom.
At each split in the path, go in the direction of the larger group of flowers.

Let's Trace the Lion's Mane

To Parents: Your child may find drawing zigzag lines difficult. Explain that he or she does not have to trace the entire mane at once. Tracing the line neatly is more important than tracing it quickly.

Trace the line around the lion's mane using any color you like. Can you roar like a lion?

• Example •

Let's Catch the Butterflies

To Parents: Guide your child to count the butterflies at the starting point. Then, make sure he or she counts the butterflies in each group before choosing which path to take.

Count the butterflies at the start of the maze. Then, draw a path from ➡ to ➡.
At each split in the path, go in the direction that has the same number of butterflies as the group at the start of the maze.

Let's Find the Animals

To Parents: In this activity, your child will use his or her observational skills to find hidden objects. If he or she does not see them right away, point out the example in the drawing below.

Can you find 3 fish and 3 birds hidden in the picture? Draw circles around them.

Let's Compare the Amounts

To Parents: In this activity, your child will compare amounts. Make sure your child knows she or he should be comparing the other objects to the dogs.

 Sticker

Count the dogs. Then, count the bones and the bowls.

Place a sticker in the ☐ next to the group that is bigger than the dogs.

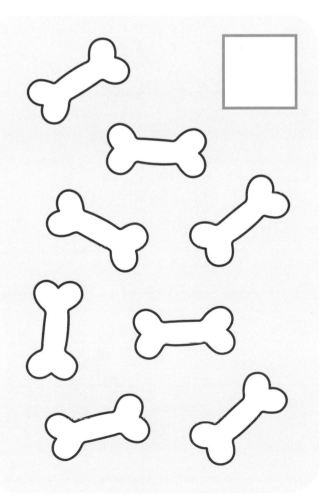

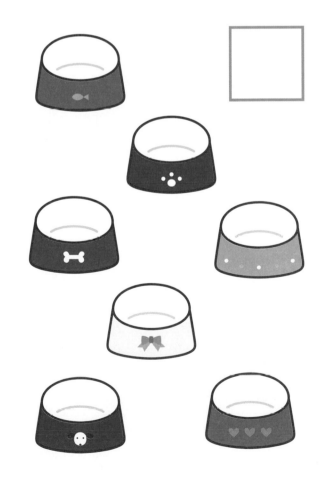

Let's Connect Quantities With Numbers

To Parents: This activity links groups of objects with numbers. If your child has difficulty matching each quantity of hamsters to its number, then have him or her count the flowers under each number and match the number of hamsters to the same number of flowers.

GOOD JOB!
Sticker

Count the hamsters in each box. Then, draw a line to connect each quantity with the matching number.

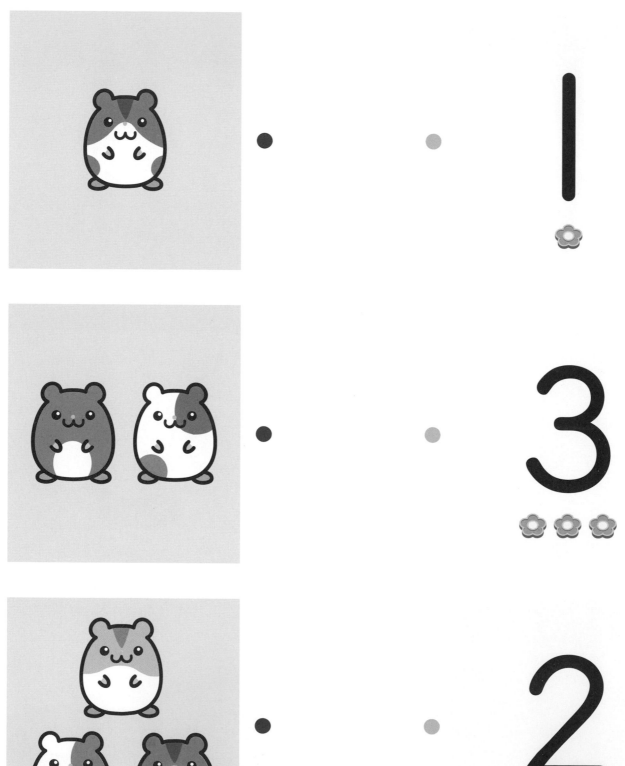

Let's Count the Turtles

To Parents: If your child is not ready to count to 10, have him or her draw a circle around the turtles one at a time. After circling each turtle, your child should color in a circle at the bottom of the page. When all the turtles are circled, help your child count the colored-in circles.

Count the turtles. Then, color the same number of ◯ at the bottom of the page. Use any color you like.

58

Let's Color by Number

To Parents: Have your child make a small mark on each area that has a 5 before coloring it in fully.

GOOD JOB!

Sticker

Find all the shapes that have a ^{FIVE} 5 . Color them using any color you like.

Let's Connect the Dots

To Parents: Encourage your child to say the numbers out loud while connecting the dots in order. Help your child with any numbers she or he does not know.

Connect the ● from with a line.

ONE	TWO	THREE	FOUR	FIVE	SIX	SEVEN	EIGHT	NINE	TEN
1 →	2 →	3 →	4 →	5 →	6 →	7 →	8 →	9 →	10

60

Let's Line Up the Ants

Place the number stickers in the ☐ to line up the ants in order, from 1 to 10.

Let's Match the Dogs

To Parents: This page is about matching quantities. Have your child count all the dogs before she or he begins. If it helps, encourage your child to write the number of dogs next to each group.

Which groups have the same number of dogs? Count the dogs in each group.
Then, draw a line from ● to ● to connect the groups.

Let's Match the Butterflies

To Parents: Encourage your child to count the number of butterflies in each group before he or she begins matching the groups.

Which groups have the same number of butterflies? Count the butterflies in each group. Then, draw a line from ● to ● to connect the groups.

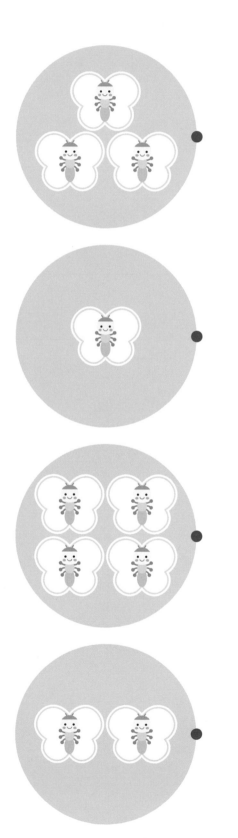

Let's Make a Snake

To Parents: It may be easier for your child to cut along the curved lines if you cut the snake out of the white background first. If you see that your child is struggling, remind him or her to turn the paper while cutting.

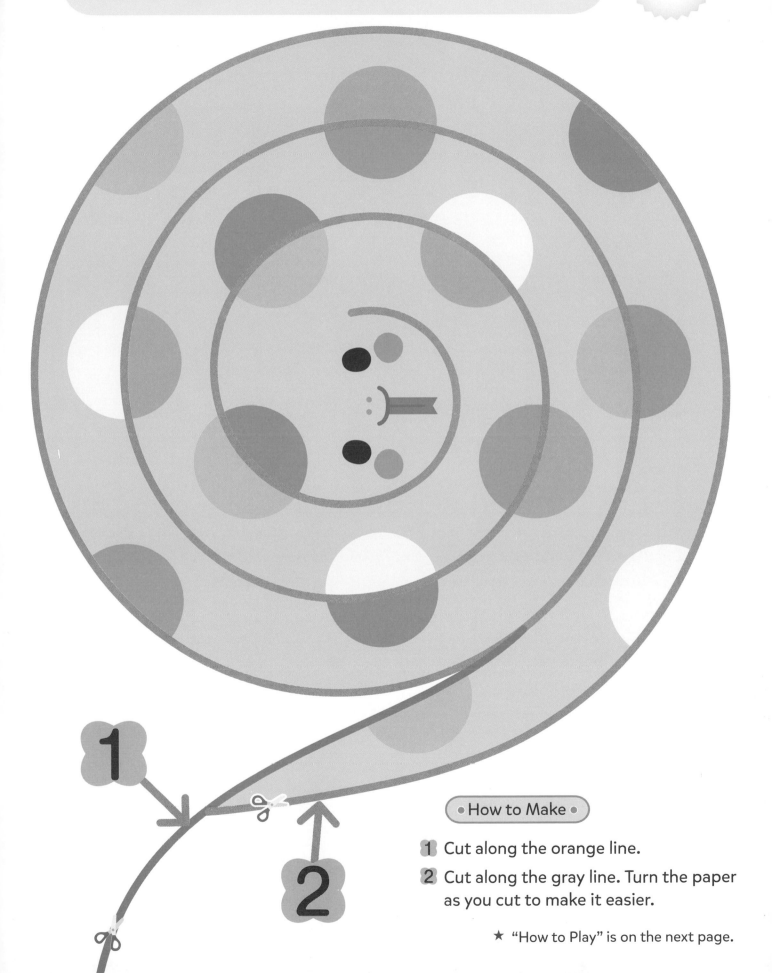

• How to Make •

1 Cut along the orange line.

2 Cut along the gray line. Turn the paper as you cut to make it easier.

★ "How to Play" is on the next page.

• How to Play •

Hold the snake by the head. Move your arm
up and down to make the snake move.

Game Board
You can write and erase again and again.

To Parents: Use water-based markers on the wipe-clean side of the board. Explain that the pictures in the example box are for ideas only and shouldn't be copied exactly. When your child is finished drawing, erase the board with a damp cloth.

Draw an animal face using the ⬭. Use your imagination!

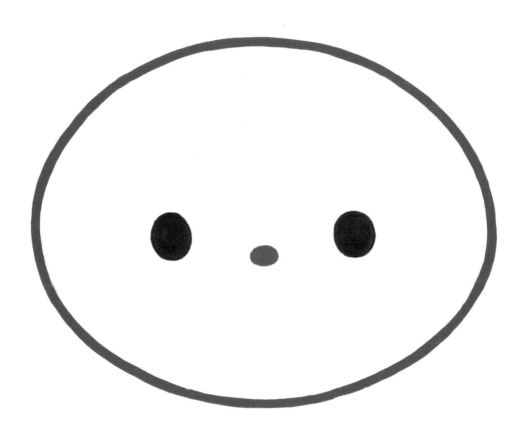

Examples

Lion   Panda   Raccoon

Bear   Tiger   Rabbit   Koala

Let's Find the Sea Creatures

To Parents: Help your child name each type of animal in the picture (turtle, octopus, squid, crab, fish). Show your child the boxes at the bottom of the page. Make sure he or she understands that the numbers in the boxes tell how many of each animal are in the picture.

The sea creatures are hiding! Can you find them all?
How many of each type of animal do you see?

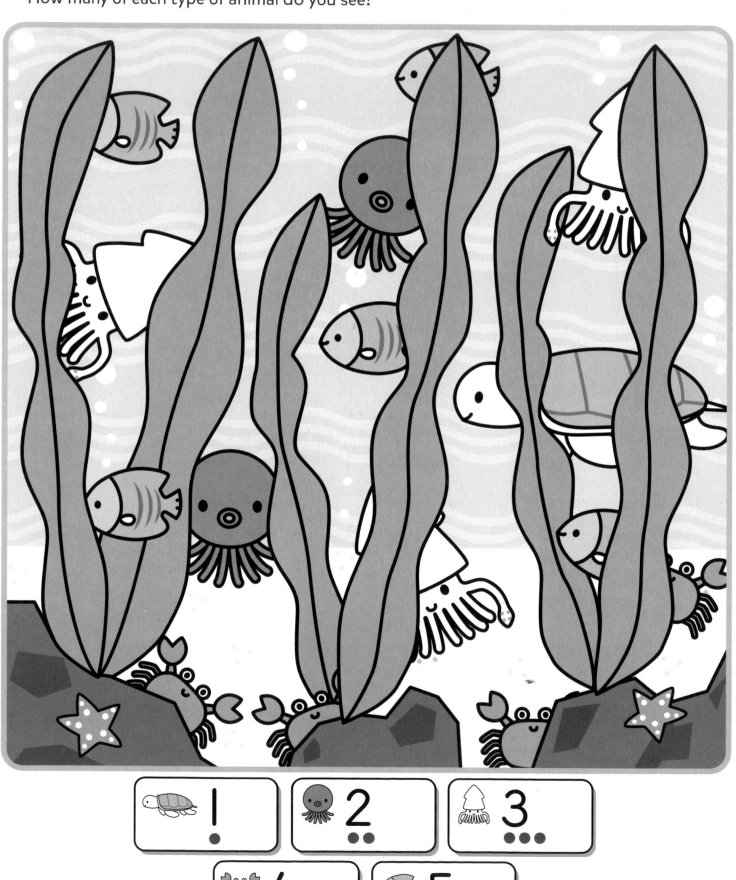